DISCARD

W9-BWH-481

PANDAS

3 1389 01894 0171

by Kathleen Pohl

Reading consultant: Susan Nations, M.Ed., author/literacy coach/ consultant in literacy development

WEEKLY READER®
PUBLISHING

Please visit our web site at: **www.garethstevens.com**
For a free color catalog describing our list of high-quality
books, call 1-800-542-2595 (USA) or 1-800-387-3178 (Canada).

Library of Congress Cataloging-in-Publication Data

Pohl, Kathleen.
    Pandas / Kathleen Pohl.
       p. cm. — (Animals I see at the zoo)
    Includes bibliographical references and index.
    ISBN 978-0-8368-8220-9 (lib. bdg.)
    ISBN 978-0-8368-8227-8 (softcover)
    1. Giant Panda—Juvenile literature. I. Title.
QL737.C27P635   2007
599.789—dc22   2007006039

This edition first published in 2008 by
Weekly Reader® Books
An imprint of Gareth Stevens Publishing
1 Reader's Digest Road
Pleasantville, NY 10570-7000 USA

Copyright © 2008 by Gareth Stevens, Inc.

Editor: Dorothy L. Gibbs
Art direction: Tammy West
Graphic designer: Charlie Dahl
Photo research: Diane Laska-Swanke

Photo credits: Cover, p. 17 © Taylor S. Kennedy/National Geographic Image Collection;
title, pp. 9, 13, 15 © Tom and Pat Leeson; p. 5 © Aaron Ferster/Photo Researchers, Inc.;
p. 7 © Bruce Davidson/naturepl.com; p. 11 © Peter Oxford/naturepl.com; p. 19 © Lynn M.
Stone/naturepl.com; p. 21 © Jessie Cohen/Smithsonian's National Zoo/CNP/CORBIS

All rights reserved. No part of this book may be reproduced, stored in a retrieval system,
or transmitted in any form or by any means, electronic, mechanical, photocopying, recording,
or otherwise without the prior written permission of the copyright holder.

Printed in the United States of America

1 2 3 4 5 6 7 8 9 11 10 09 08 07

Note to Educators and Parents

Reading is such an exciting adventure for young children! They are beginning to integrate their oral language skills with written language. To encourage children along the path to early literacy, books must be colorful, engaging, and interesting; they should invite the young reader to explore both the print and the pictures.

The *Animals I See at the Zoo* series is designed to help children read about the fascinating animals they might see at a zoo. In each book, young readers will learn interesting facts about the featured animal.

Each book is specially designed to support the young reader in the reading process. The familiar topics are appealing to young children and invite them to read — and re-read — again and again. The full-color photographs and enhanced text further support the student during the reading process.

In addition to serving as wonderful picture books in schools, libraries, homes, and other places where children learn to love reading, these books are specifically intended to be read within an instructional guided reading group. This small group setting allows beginning readers to work with a fluent adult model as they make meaning from the text. After children develop fluency with the text and content, the books can be read independently. Children and adults alike will find these books supportive, engaging, and fun!

— Susan Nations, M.Ed., author, literacy coach,
and consultant in literacy development

I like to go to the zoo. I see **pandas** at the zoo.

Did you know a panda is not a bear? It just looks like a bear.

Pandas are
black and white.
They have white
faces with black
ears and black
eye patches.

eye patches

Pandas eat a lot!
They eat tall grass
called **bamboo**.
In zoos, pandas
eat apples and
carrots, too.

bamboo

They hold their food with their paws. Their front paws work like hands.

The sharp **claws** on their paws help pandas climb trees.

claws

Pandas like to sleep in trees.

Pandas come from **China**, but only a few still live there. Zoos keep pandas safe.

I like to see
pandas at the
zoo. Do you?

Glossary

bamboo — tall, hollow grass that grows in warm climates

China — a huge country in Asia

claws — the sharp, curved "toenails" on a panda's paws

pandas — animals from China that have thick, black-and-white fur and that look like bears

For More Information

Books

Arnold, Caroline. *Caroline Arnold's Animals: A Panda's World*. Mankato, Minnesota: Coughlan Publishing, Picture Window Books, 2006.

Bredeson, Carmen. *Zoom in on Animals! Giant Pandas Up Close*. Berkeley Heights, New Jersey: Enslow Elementary, 2006.

Ryder, Joanne. *Little Panda: The World Welcomes Hua Mei at the San Diego Zoo*. New York: Simon & Schuster, Aladdin, 2004

Web Site
Panda Kids

www.pandaexpress.com/pandakids/
html/fun_facts/index.html
Find fun facts, photos, games, quizzes, and lots more.

Publisher's note to educators and parents: Our editors have carefully reviewed this Web site to ensure that it is suitable for children. Many Web sites change frequently, however, and we cannot guarantee that a site's future contents will continue to meet our high standards of quality and educational value. Be advised that children should be closely supervised whenever they access the Internet.

Index

About the Author

Kathleen Pohl has written and edited many children's books, including animal tales, rhyming books, retold classics, and the forty-book series *Nature Close-Ups*. Most recently, she authored the Weekly Reader® leveled reader series *Let's Read About Animals* and *Where People Work*. She also served for many years as top editor of *Taste of Home* and *Country Woman* magazines. She and her husband, Bruce, share their home in the beautiful Wisconsin woods with six goats, a llama, and all kinds of wonderful woodland creatures.

Animals I See at the Zoo

RHINOS

DISCARD

3 1389 01894 0288

by Kathleen Pohl

Reading consultant: Susan Nations, M.Ed., author/literacy coach/ consultant in literacy development

WEEKLY READER®
PUBLISHING

Please visit our web site at: www.garethstevens.com
For a free color catalog describing our list of high-quality
books, call 1-800-542-2595 (USA) or 1-800-387-3178 (Canada).

Library of Congress Cataloging-in-Publication Data

Pohl, Kathleen.
    Rhinos / Kathleen Pohl.
        p. cm. — (Animals I see at the zoo)
    Includes bibliographical references and index.
    ISBN 978-0-8368-8222-3 (lib. bdg.)
    ISBN 978-0-8368-8229-2 (softcover)
    1. Rhinoceroses—Juvenile literature. I. Title.
    QL737.U63P64   2008
    599.66'8—dc22   2007006042

Copyright © 2008 by Gareth Stevens, Inc.

This edition first published in 2008 by
Weekly Reader® Books
An imprint of Gareth Stevens Publishing
1 Reader's Digest Road
Pleasantville, NY 10570-7000 USA

Editor: Dorothy L. Gibbs
Art direction: Tammy West
Graphic designer: Charlie Dahl
Photo research: Diane Laska-Swanke

Photo credits: Cover © Roy Toft/National Geographic Image Collection;
title © Diane Laska-Swanke; pp. 5, 9, 15, 17, 19, 21 © James P. Rowan;
p. 7 © Bernard Castelein/naturepl.com; p. 11 © Sven-Olof Lindblad/Photo
Researchers, Inc.; p. 13 Thomas A. Hermann/NBII

All rights reserved. No part of this book may be reproduced, stored in a retrieval system,
or transmitted in any form or by any means, electronic, mechanical, photocopying, recording,
or otherwise without the prior written permission of the copyright holder.

Printed in the United States of America

1 2 3 4 5 6 7 8 9 11 10 09 08 07